Superstitions

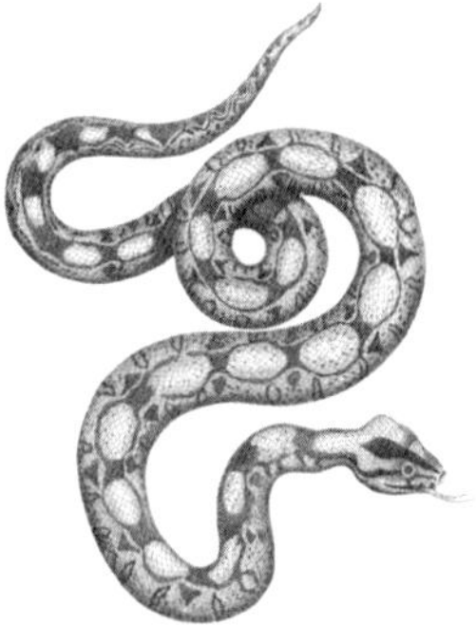

Superstitions

Omens, Charms, Cures 1787

From an original text by Francis Grose

Introduction by John Simpson

Bodleian Library
UNIVERSITY OF OXFORD

First printed in 1787 for S. Hooper, London, as *A provincial glossary, with a collection of local proverbs, and popular superstitions*, by Francis Grose. Italicization has been left as per the original version

This edition first published in 2011 by the Bodleian Library
Broad Street
Oxford OX1 3BG

www.bodleianbookshop.co.uk

ISBN: 978 1 85124 286 3

Introduction © John Simpson 2011

All rights reserved

No part of this book may be reproduced, stored in a retrieval system, or transmitted in any form or by any means, electronic, mechanical, photocopying, recording, or otherwise, without the written permission of the Bodleian Library, except for the purpose of research or private study, or criticism or review.

Cover design by Dot Little
Designed and typeset in georgia font (9.5pt on 11.7pt)
by JCS Publishing Services Ltd,
www.jcs-publishing.co.uk
Printed and bound in China by C&C Offset Printing Co. Ltd
on 100gsm YuLong pure 1.3

British Library Catalogue in Publishing Data
A CIP record of this publication is available from the British Library

Contents

Introduction	7
Superstitions	11
A Ghost	17
A Witch	31
A Sorcerer, or Magician	50
Fairies	58
The Second-Sight	63
Omens Portending Death	69
Charms and Ceremonies for Knowing Future Events	75
Superstitious Cures and Preventatives	79
Sympathy	83
Things Lucky and Unlucky	84
Miscellaneous Superstitions	93

Introduction

FRANCIS GROSE WAS known to his contemporaries as a celebrated antiquarian, the author of several important works such as *The Antiquities of England and Wales* (1772–87) and *A Treatise on Ancient Armour* (1785-7). His antiquarian work has nowadays of course been superseded and he is principally remembered today, especially amongst lexicographers and historians of language, for his two dictionaries: *A Classical Dictionary of the Vulgar Tongue* (1785) and *A Provincial Glossary, with a Collection of Local Proverbs, and Popular Superstitions* (1787).

Superstitions—published here separately for the first time—is the sparking tail-piece to the *Provincial Glossary*. Grose's scholarly predecessors tended to focus on 'superstition' in the grand sense: 'belief in a religion considered false or pagan', 'religious belief or practice founded on fear or ignorance', citing the classical authors on the subject. Grose adjusted his vista to the local and the familiar; he writes engaging and surprisingly structured essays on ghosts and witches and sorcerers, before turning his attention to sequences of individual superstitions. He is the first cited reference in English, in Opie and Tatem's *Oxford Dictionary of Superstitions* (1989), for the advice not to walk under ladders.

Francis Grose was born Francis Gross, the eldest son of the Swiss-born jeweller Francis Gross (later Grose) and his wife Anne, of the City of London and later of Richmond, Surrey. He is first encountered with the British army in Flanders in early 1747, but he spent most of his life as a member of the Surrey Militia, rising to the rank of captain in 1765. In 1755 his father bought him the position of Richmond herald at the London College of Arms, but he seems not to have found the work congenial (although as herald he would have attended the coronation of George III), and he sold the position in 1763. To his contemporaries he was almost universally 'Captain Grose'. Grose says that his travels around the British Isles with the militia gave him the opportunity to collect material for his *Antiquities* and for his lexicographical works.

He was a talented draughtsman, and his antiquarian publications are lavishly illustrated with his engravings. In later life he was known for his great girth: he joked that he was wider than he was tall. But as a companion he was regarded as second to none (not least by Burns). His principal failing was his inability to handle money—unfortunate as he was paymaster for his militia unit. He got into serious debt to his fellow officers in the 1780s, despite having earlier received substantial bequests from the wills of his parents and wife. It seems that it was his indebtedness that caused him to broaden the scope of his writings in later life.

Superstitions only benefits from this. Grose writes as an enlightened rationalist, both embracing his subject and examining it at arm's length. He enumerates the attributes of ghosts as if he believes in them (are they always white?); he tells us crisply about seventh sons of seventh sons, about witches' cats, and the stones in the heads of toads. The *Encyclopaedia Britannica* liked his essay on ghosts so much that the editors quoted it wholesale in their 1791 edition. We need to spend some more time with Francis Grose.

John Simpson
Oxford

Superstitions

It will scarcely be conceived how great a number of superstitious notions and practices are still remaining and prevalent in different parts of these kingdoms, many of which are still used and alluded to even in and about the metropolis; and every person, however carefully educated, will, upon examination, find that he has some how or other imbibed and stored up in his memory a much greater number of these rules and maxims than he could at first have imagined.

To account for this, we need only turn our recollection towards what passed in our childhood, and reflect on the avidity and pleasure with which we listened to stories of ghosts, witches, and fairies, told us by our maids and nurses. And even among those whose parents had the good sense to prohibit such relations, there is scarce one in a thousand but may remember to have heard, from some maiden aunt or antiquated cousin, the various omens that have announced the approaching deaths of different branches of the family; a copious catalogue of things lucky and unlucky; a variety of charms to cure warts, the cramp, and tooth-ach; preventatives against the nightmare; with observations relative to sympathy, denoted by shiverings, burning of the cheeks, and itchings of the eyes and elbows. The effects of ideas of this kind are not easily got the better of; and the ideas themselves rarely, if ever, forgotten.

In former times these notions were so prevalent, that it was deemed little less than atheism to doubt them; and in many instances the terrors caused by them embittered the lives of a great number of persons of all ages, by degrees almost shutting them out of their own houses, and deterring them from going from one village to another after sun-set. The room in which the head of a family had died, was for a long time untenanted; particularly if they died without a will, or were supposed to have entertained any particular religious opinions.

But if any disconsolate old maiden, or love-crossed bachelor, happened to dispatch themselves in their garters, the room where the deed was perpetrated was rendered for ever after uninhabitable, and not unfrequently was nailed up. If a drunken farmer, returning from market, fell from Old Dobbin and broke his neck—or a carter, under the same predicament, tumbled from his cart or waggon, and was killed by it—that spot was ever after haunted and impassable: in short, there was scarcely a bye-lane or cross-way but had its ghost, who appeared in the shape of a headless cow or horse; or, clothed all in white, glared with its saucer eyes over a gate or stile. Ghosts of superior rank, when they appeared abroad, rode in coaches drawn by six headless horses, and driven by a headless coachman and postilions. Almost every ancient manorhouse was haunted by some one at least of its former masters or mistresses, where, besides diverse other noises, that of telling money was distinctly heard: and as for the churchyards, the number of ghosts that walked there, according to the village computation, almost equalled the living parishioners: to pass them at night, was an achievement not to be attempted by any one in the parish, the sextons excepted, who perhaps being particularly privileged, to make use of the common expression, never saw any thing worse than themselves.

Terrible and inconvenient as these matters might be, they were harmless, compared with the horrid consequences attending the belief of witchcraft, which, to the eternal disgrace of this country, even made its way into our courts of judicature, and pervaded and poisoned the minds of the judges: and it is with a mixture of shame, remorse, and indignation, that we read of hundreds of poor innocent persons who fell victims to this ridiculous opinion, and who were regularly murdered under the sanction of, and with all the forms of, the law. Sometimes, by the combination of wicked and artful persons, these notions were made stalking horses to interest and revenge.

The combinations here alluded to, were practised by some popish priests during the reign of King James I. who was himself a believer in witchcraft. These priests, in order to advance the interest of their religion, or rather their own emolument, pretended to have the power of casting out devils from demoniacs and persons bewitched; and for this purpose suborned some artful and idle youths and wenches to act the part of persons bewitched, and to suffer themselves to be dispossessed by their prayers, and sprinklings with holy water. In order to perform these parts, they were to counterfeit violent fits and convulsions, on signs given them; and, in compliance with the popular notions, to vomit up crooked nails, pins, needles, coals, and other rubbish, privately conveyed to them. It was, besides, necessary to accuse some person of having bewitched them; a poor superannuated man, or peevish old woman, was therefore pitched on, whose detection, indictment, and execution, were to terminate the villany. Luckily these combinations were at length discovered and exposed; but it must make the blood of every humane person thrill with horror, to hear that in New England there were at one time upwards of three hundred persons all imprisoned for witchcraft. Confuted and ridiculed as these opinions have lately been, the seeds of them still remain in the mind, and at different times have attempted to spring forth; witness the Cock-lane Ghost, and the disturbance at Stockwell. Indeed it is within these very few years that witchcraft has been erased from among the crimes cognizable by a jury.

In order to give a methodical view of the different kinds of Superstition now and formerly current in this country, I shall arrange my subject under the following heads: Ghosts—Witches, Sorcerers, and Witchcraft—Fairies—Corps, Candles, &c.—Second Sight—Omens—Things lucky and unlucky—Spells, Charms, and other fanciful devices for preventing and curing Disorders—Superstitious Methods of obtaining a Knowledge of Future Events—Sympathy—and Miscellaneous Superstitions.

A Ghost

A GHOST IS SUPPOSED to be the spirit of a person deceased, who is either commissioned to return for some special errand, such as the discovery of a murder, to procure restitution of lands or money unjustly withheld from an orphan or widow—or, having committed some injustice whilst living, cannot rest till that is redressed. Sometimes the occasion of spirits revisiting this world, is to inform their heir in what secret place, or private drawer in an old trunk, they had hidden the title deeds of the estate; or where, in troublesome times, they buried their money or plate. Some Ghosts of murdered persons, whose bodies have been secretly buried, cannot be at ease till their bones have been taken up, and deposited in consecrated ground, with all the rites of Christian burial. This idea is the remains of a very old piece of Heathen Superstition: The Ancients believed that Charon was not permitted to ferry over the Ghosts of unburied persons, but that they wandered up and down the banks of the river Styx for an hundred years, after which they were admitted to a passage. This is mentioned by Virgil:

> Haec omnis quam cernis, inops inhumataque turba est:
> Portitor ille, Charon; hi quos vehit unda, sepulti.
> Nec ripas datur horrendas, nec rauca fluenta,
> Transportare prius quam sedibus offa quiêrunt.

Centum errant annos, volitant que haec
    littora circum:
Tum, demum admissi, stagna exoptata
    revisunt.

Sometimes Ghosts appear in consequence of an agreement made, whilst living, with some particular friend, that he who first died should appear to the survivor.

Glanvil tells us of the Ghost of a person who had lived but a disorderly kind of life, for which it was condemned to wander up and down the earth, in the company of evil spirits, till the day of judgment.

In most of the relations of Ghosts, they are supposed to be mere aërial beings, without substance, and that they can pass through walls and other solid bodies at pleasure. A particular instance of this is given, in Relation the 27th, in Glanvil's Collection, where one David Hunter, neat-herd to the Bishop of Down and Connor, was for a long time haunted by the apparition of an old woman, whom he was by a secret impulse obliged to follow whenever she appeared, which he says he did for a considerable time, even if in bed with his wife: and because his wife could not hold him in his bed, she would go too, and walk after him till day, though she saw nothing; but his little dog was so well acquainted with the apparition, that he would follow it as well as his master. If a tree stood in her walk, he observed her always to go through it.—Notwithstanding this seeming immateriality, this very Ghost was not without some substance; for, having performed her errand, she desired Hunter to lift her from the ground; in the doing of which, he says, she felt just like a bag of feathers.—We sometimes also read of Ghosts striking violent blows; and that, if not made way for, they overturn all impediments, like a furious whirlwind. Glanvil mentions an instance of this, in Relation 17th, of a Dutch lieutenant, who had the faculty of seeing Ghosts; and who, being prevented making way for one which he mentioned to some friends as coming towards them, was, with his companions, violently thrown down, and sorely bruised. We further learn, by Relation 16th, that the hand of a Ghost is 'as cold as a clod.'

The usual time at which Ghosts make their appearance is midnight, and seldom before it is dark; though some audacious spirits have been said to appear even by day-light: but of this there are few instances, and those mostly Ghosts who have been laid, perhaps in the Red Sea (of which more hereafter), and whose times of confinement were expired: these, like felons confined to the lighters, are said to return more troublesome and daring than before. No Ghosts can appear on Christmas eve; this Shakespeare has put into the mouth of one of his characters in Hamlet.

Ghosts commonly appear in the same dress they usually wore whilst living, though they are sometimes clothed all in white; but that is chiefly the churchyard Ghosts, who have no particular business, but seem to appear *pro bono publico*, or to scare drunken rustics from tumbling over their graves.

I cannot learn that Ghosts carry tapers in their hands, as they are sometimes depicted, though the room in which they appear, is without fire or candle, is frequently said to be as light as day. Dragging chains, is not the fashion of English Ghosts; chains and black vestments being chiefly the accoutrements of foreign spectres, seen in arbitrary governments: dead or alive, English spirits are free. One instance, however, of an English Ghost dressed in black, is found in the celebrated ballad of William and Margaret, in the following lines:

> And clay-cold was her lily hand.
> That held her *sable shrowd*.

This, however, may be considered as a poetical licence, used in all likelihood for the sake of the opposition of *lily* to *sable*.

If, during the time of an apparition, there is a lighted candle in the room, it will burn extremely blue: this is so universally acknowledged, that many eminent philosophers have busied themselves in accounting for it, without once doubting the truth of the fact. Dogs too have the faculty of seeing spirits, as is instanced in David Hunter's relation, above quoted; but in that case they usually shew signs of terror, by whining and creeping to their master for protection: and it is generally supposed that they often see things of this nature when their owner cannot; there being some persons, particularly those born on a Christmas eve, who cannot see spirits.

The coming of a spirit is announced some time before its appearance, by a variety of loud and dreadful noises; sometimes rattling in the old hall like a coach and six, and rumbling up and down the stair-case like the trundling of bowls or cannon balls. At length the door flies open, and the spectre stalks slowly up to the bed's foot, and opening the curtains, looks stedfastly at the person in bed by whom it is seen; a ghost being very rarely visible to more than one person, although there are several in company. It is here necessary to observe, that it has been universally found by experience, as well as affirmed by diverse apparitions themselves, that a Ghost has not the power to speak till it has been first spoken to; so that, notwithstanding the urgency of the business on which it may come, every thing must stand still till the person visited can find sufficient courage to speak to it: an event that sometimes does not take place for many years. It has not been found that female Ghosts are more loquacious than those of the male sex, both being equally restrained by this law.

The mode of addressing a Ghost is by commanding it, in the name of the Three Persons of the Trinity, to tell you who it is, and what is its business: this it may be necessary to repeat three times; after which it will, in a low and hollow voice, declare its satisfaction at being spoken to, and desire the party addressing it not to be afraid, for it will do him no harm. This being premised, it commonly enters into its narrative, which being completed, and its request or commands given, with injunctions that they be immediately executed, it vanishes away, frequently in a flash of light; in which case, some Ghosts have been so considerate as to desire the party to whom they appeared to shut their eyes: sometimes its departure is attended with delightful music. During the narration of its business, a Ghost must by no means be interrupted by questions of any kind; so doing is extremely dangerous: if any doubts arise, they must be stated after the spirit has done its tale. Questions respecting its state, or the state of any of their former acquaintance, are offensive, and not often answered; spirits, perhaps, being restrained from divulging the secrets of their prison house. Occasionally spirits will even condescend to talk on common occurrences, as is instanced by Glanvil in the apparition of

Major George Sydenham to Captain William Dyke, Relation 10th, wherein the Major reproved the Captain for suffering a sword he had given him to grow rusty; saying, 'Captain, Captain, this sword did not use to be kept after this manner when it was mine.' This attention to the state of arms, was a remnant of the Major's professional duty when living.

It is somewhat remarkable that Ghosts do not go about their business like the persons of this world. In cases of murder, a Ghost, instead of going to the next justice of the peace, and laying its information, or to the nearest relation of the person murdered, appears to some poor labourer who knows none of the parties, draws the curtains of some decrepit nurse or alms-woman, or hovers about the place where his body is deposited. The same circuitous mode is pursued with respect to redressing injured orphans or widows; when it seems as if the shortest and most certain way would be, to go to the person guilty of the injustice, and haunt him continually till he be terrified into a restitution. Nor are the pointing out lost writings generally managed in a more summary way; the Ghost commonly applying to a third person, ignorant of the whole affair, and a stranger to all concerned.—But it is presumptuous to scrutinize too far into these matters: Ghosts have undoubtedly forms and customs peculiar to themselves.

If, after the first appearance, the persons employed neglect, or are prevented from, performing the message or business committed to their management, the Ghost appears continually to them, at first with a discontented, next an angry, and at length with a furious countenance, threatening to tear them in pieces if the matter is not forthwith executed; sometimes terrifying them, as in Glanvil's Relation 26th, by appearing in many formidable shapes, and sometimes even striking them a violent blow. Of blows given by Ghosts there are many instances, and some wherein they have been followed with an incurable lameness.

It should have been observed that Ghosts, in delivering their commissions, in order to ensure belief, communicate to the persons employed some secret, known only to the parties concerned and themselves, the relation of which always produces the effect intended.—The business being completed, Ghosts appear with a cheerful countenance, saying they shall now be at rest, and will never more disturb any one; and, thanking their agents, by way of reward communicate to them something relative to themselves, which they will never reveal.

Sometimes Ghosts appear, and disturb a house, without deigning to give any reason for so doing: with these, the shortest and only way is to exorcise, and eject them; or, as the vulgar term is, lay them. For this purpose there must be two or three clergymen, and the ceremony must be performed in Latin; a language that strikes the most audacious Ghost with terror. A Ghost may be laid for any term less than an hundred years, and in any place or body, full or empty; as, a solid oak—the pommel of a sword—a barrel of beer, if a yeoman or simple gentleman—or a pipe of wine, if an esquire or a justice. But of all places the most common, and what a Ghost least likes, is the Red Sea; it being related, in many instances, that Ghosts have most earnestly besought the exorcists not to confine them in that place. It is nevertheless considered as an indisputable fact, that there are an infinite number laid there, perhaps from its being a safer prison than any other nearer at hand; though neither history nor tradition gives us any instance of Ghosts escaping or returning from this kind of transportation before their time.

Having thus given the most striking outlines of the popular Superstitions respecting

Ghosts, I shall next treat of another species of human apparition, which, though it something resemble it, does not come under the description of a Ghost, These are the exact figures and resemblances of persons then living, often seen not only by their friends at a distance, but many times by themselves; of which there are several instances in Aubery's Miscellanies: one, of Sir Richard Napier, a physician of London, who being on the road from Bedfordshire to visit a friend in Berkshire, saw at an inn his own apparition lying on the bed as a dead corps; he nevertheless went forward, and died in a short time: another, of Lady Diana Rich, daughter of the Earl of Holland, who met her own apparition walking in a garden at Kensington, and died a month after of the small-pox. These apparitions are called Fetches, and in Cumberland, Swarths; they most commonly appear to distant friends and relations, at the very instant preceding the death of the person whose figure they put on. Sometimes, as in the instances above mentioned, there is a greater interval between the appearance and death.

A Witch

A WITCH IS ALMOST universally a poor, decrepit, superannuated, old woman, who, being in great distress, is tempted by a man clothed in a black coat or gown; sometimes, as in Scotland, wearing also a bluish band and hand-cuffs, that is, a kind of turn-up linen sleeve: this man promises her, if she will sign a contract to become his, both soul and body, she shall want for nothing, and that he will revenge her upon all her enemies. The agreement being concluded, he gives her some trifling sum of money, from half a crown down to four pence, to bind the bargain; then cutting or pricking her finger, causes her to sign her name, or make a cross as her mark, with her blood on a piece of parchment: what is the form of these contracts, is no where mentioned. In addition to this signature, in

Scotland, the Devil made the Witches put one hand to the sole of their foot, and the other to the crown of their head, thereby signifying they were entirely his. In making these bargains there is sometimes a great deal of haggling, as is instanced in the account of the negociation between Oliver Cromwell and the Devil, before the battle of Worcester, published in Echard's History of England. Before the Devil quits his new recruit, he delivers to her an imp or familiar, and sometimes two or three; they are of different shapes and forms, some resembling a cat or kitten, others a mole, a miller fly, or some other insect or animal: these are to come at her call, to do such mischief as she shall direct them; at stated times of the day they suck her blood, through teats on different parts of her body: these on inspection appear red and raw. Feeding, suckling, or rewarding these imps, was by law declared felony.

There are, it is held, three sorts of Witches. The first can hurt, but not help: these, from their diabolical qualities, are called Black Witches. The second sort can help, but not hurt: these are unhappy persons, who, for the power of curing diseases, finding stolen goods, and doing other acts of utility, for which they take money, become bond slaves to the Devil; they are at continual enmity with the Black Witches, insomuch that one or the other often fall a sacrifice to their wicked arts: these are commonly styled White Witches. The third sort are those who can both help and hurt; and, as they seem a sort of mixture between White and Black, and wanting a name, may, without any great impropriety, be named Grey Witches.

But to return to the common Witch, which seems of the black sort, we do not find that, in consequence of her wicked compact, she enjoys much of the good things of this world, but still continues in abject penury. Sometimes indeed she, in company with others of her sisterhood, are carried through the air on brooms, spits, &c. to distant meetings, or sabbaths, of Witches; but for this they must anoint themselves with a certain magical ointment, given them by the Devil.

At these meetings they have feastings, music, and dancing, the Devil himself sometimes condescending to play on the pipe, or cittern; and some of them have carnal copulation with him, the produce of which is toads and serpents: sometimes the Devil, to oblige a male Witch or Wizard, of which there are some few, puts on the shape of a woman. Mr. Sinclair tells us, in his book intitled The Invisible World, that one William Barton, who, with his wife, was burnt in Scotland for Witchcraft, confessed that he lay with the Devil in the shape of a gentlewoman, and had

fifteen pounds of him in good money; but this he again denied before his execution. His wife confessed that the Devil went before them to a dancing, in the shape of a dog, playing upon a pair of pipes; and, coming down the hill back again, he carried the candle in his bottom, under his tail, which played, *ey wig wag, wig wag:* that, she said, was almost all the pleasure she ever had. Generally, before the assembly breaks up, they all have the honour of saluting Satan's posteriors, who, for that ceremony, usually appears under the figure of a he-goat, though in Scotland it was performed when he appeared under the human form. In their way to and from these meetings, they sometimes sing or repeat certain barbarous words: in going, they use these words — *tout, tout a tout, tout tought, throughout and about*; in returning, *rentum tormentum*. In Scotland it was confessed and deposed, that, at some of these meetings, the Devil got up into the pulpit, and preached a sermon in a voice *hough* and *gustie*; and afterwards caused the Witches to open several graves, out of which they took part of the body, the joints of the fingers and toes, with some of the winding-sheet: this was to prepare a powder for magical uses.

It now and then happens that Satan, being out of humour, or for diversion, beats the Witches black and blue with the spits and brooms, the vehicles of their transportation, and plays them divers other unlucky tricks. Any one repeating the name of GOD, instantly puts the whole assembly to flight.

Here likewise the Devil distributes apples, dishes, spoons, or other trifles, to those Witches who desire to torment any particular person; these they present to them, and thereby obtain a power over them.

When a Witch wishes to destroy any one to whom she bears an ill will, she and her sister Witches make an image of wax, which, with many ceremonies, is baptized by the Devil, and named after the person meant to be injured; after which they stick thorns into it, and set it before a fire: and, as the wax melts by the heat, so the body of the person represented decays by sickness, with great torture, having the sensation of thorns stuck into his or her flesh.

On some occasions. Witches content themselves with a less cruel revenge, and only oblige the objects of their anger to swallow pins, crooked nails, dirt, cinders, and trash of all sorts, which they invisibly convey to them, or send them by their imps. Frequently they shew their spite, by drying up cows, and killing oxen; which last they have particular power to do, because, as the Apostle says. Doth God take care of oxen? 1 *Cor.* ix. 9. For any slight offence, they prevent butter from coming in the churn, or beer from working.

Witches, in vexing persons, sometimes send a number of evil spirits into them; these, as they (that is, the spirits) have informed several exorcists, are also of different ranks and degrees. In one Sarah Williams were these: Killico, Hob, and a third anonymous; Coronell Portorichio, Frateretto, Fliberdiggibbet, Horberdidance, Tocobatto, and Lusty Jolly Jenkin, Puffe and Purre, Lustie Dickie Cornerd Cappe, Nurre, Molken, Wilken, Helemodion, and Kellicocum. Besides these, there were in others Captain Pippen, Captain Philpot, Captain Maho, and Captain Soforce: these were all leaders. There were also sometimes, with these Captains, divers private spirits; as in a Mr. Trayford there were, Hilco, Smalkin,

Hillio, Hiachto, and Lustie Huff Cap: all these may be found in a book intitled Egregious Popish Impostures, &c. practised by Edmunds, alias Wefton, a Jesuit, &c. published in 1603, p. 49, 50.

One Mother Samuel, the Witch of Warbois, had nine spirits that belonged to her and her family; two of their names arc forgotten, but those of the other seven were *Pluck*, Hardname, Catch—three of the name of *Smack*, who were cousins—and one called Blew. These spirits used to converse freely with the children of Mr. Throgmorton, whose house they troubled. The following was a dialogue which passed between the eldest daughter, a girl of about seventeen, and one of the Smacks, whom she supposed in love with her.—'From whence come you, Mr. Smack, and what news do you bring?' The spirit answered that 'he came from fighting.'—'From fighting!' said she; 'with whom, I pray you?' The spirit answered, 'With Pluck'—'Where did you fight, I pray?' said she.

The spirit answered, 'In his old dame's backhouse,'—which is an old house standing in Mother Samuel's yard; and they fought with great cowl staves this last night.—'And who got the mastery, I pray you?' says she. He answered, 'that he broke Pluck's head.'—Said she, 'I would that he had broke your neck also.' Saith the spirit, 'Is that all the thanks I shall have for my labour?'—'Why,' saith she, 'do you look for thanks at my hand? I would you were all hanged up, one against another, and Dame and all, for you are all naught: but it is no matter,' said she; 'I do not well to curse you, for God, I trust, will defend me from you all.'—So he departed, and bade farewell.—Soon after, she sees Pluck coming with his head hanging down; and he told her again of the battle, and how his head was broke. When he was gone, Catch, she said, came limping with a broken leg; and, after him, Blew brought his arm in a string: but they threatened that, when they should be well, they would join together, and be revenged of *Smack*. Next time that Smack came, she told him of their design; but he set them at light: he bragged that he could beat two of them himself, and his cousin Smack would be on his side.

I will not tire the Reader with any more of this miserable nonsense; but what can we think of a court of judicature, that would permit such stuff to be repeated before them as evidence? Nevertheless this, and such like, was deemed sufficient to condemn a man, his wife, and daughter, who were all executed. The old woman, it is said, confessed her guilt; but it is likewise believed she was, at that time, from the vexation, and experiments she had undergone by way of trial, rendered insane.

Frequently Witches, in vexing the parties troubled, were visible to them only; and, when they have struck at them with a knife, or other weapon, the Witches have been found to have received a hurt in the part where their apparitions were struck.

Scratching or pricking a Witch, so as to draw blood of her, prevents her having any power over the person that does it, provided it is done before any spell has taken place: and it may be done by proxy, for one's child; provided, at the time, it is said to be done on the child's account, or for its sake.

Witches, perhaps for the sake of air and exercise, or to vex the squire, justice, and parson of the village wherein they reside, often transform themselves into hares, and lead the hounds and huntsman a long and fruitless chase; though this is sometimes attended with danger to themselves, as appears from the account of the trial of Julian Cox, published by Glanvil;

wherein it was deposed, by the huntsman, that, having chased a hare till it was fairly run down, he stept before the hounds to take it up; when, to his great amazement, instead of a hare, he found old Julian! breathless, and grovelling on the earth, with her *globes* upwards; for so he termed her backside.

There are various experiments and trials for discovering a Witch. One, by weighing her against the church Bible, which, if she is guilty, will preponderate: another, by making her attempt to say the Lord's Prayer; this no Witch is able to repeat entirely, but will omit some part or sentence thereof. It is remarkable, that all Witches do not hesitate at the same place; some leaving out one part, and some another.

Teats, through which the imps suck, are indubitable marks of a Witch: these, as has been before observed, are always raw, and also insensible; and, if squeezed, sometimes yield a drop of blood.

A witch cannot weep more than three tears, and that only out of the left eye: this want of tears was, by the witch-finders, and even by some judges, considered as a very substantial proof of guilt.

Swimming a Witch, is another kind of popular ordeal generally practised: for this, she must be stripped naked, and cross bound, the right thumb to the left toe, and the left thumb to the right toe: thus prepared, she is thrown into a pond or river, in which, if guilty, she cannot sink; for having, by her compact with the Devil, renounced the benefit of the water of baptism, that element, in its turn, renounces her, and refuses to receive her into its bosom.

Sir Robert Filmer mentions two others, by fire: the first, by burning the thatch of the house of the suspected Witch; the other, burning any animal supposed to be bewitched by her, as a hog or ox: these, it was held, would force a Witch to confess.

The trial by the stool, was another method used for the discovery of Witches; it was thus managed: Having taken the suspected Witch, she is placed in the middle of a room, upon a stool or table, cross-legged, or in some other uneasy posture; to which if she submits not, she is then bound with cords: there is she watched, and kept without meat or sleep, for the space of four-and-twenty hours (for, they say, within that time they shall see her imp come and suck). A little hole is likewise made in the door, for imps to come in at; and lest it should come in some less discernible shape, they that watch are taught to be ever and anon sweeping the room, and, if they see any spiders or flies, to kill them; and, if they cannot kill them, then they may be sure they are imps.

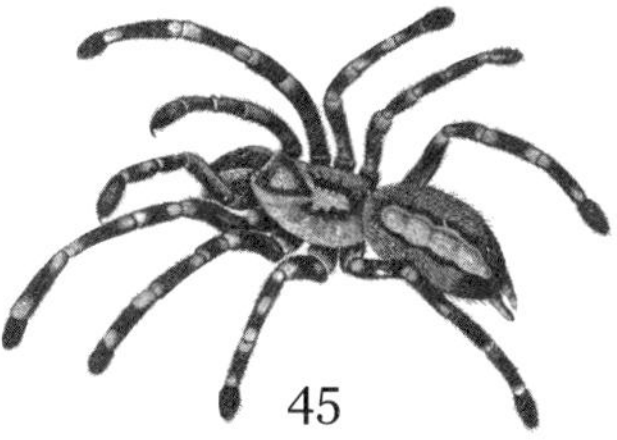

If Witches, under examination or torture, will not confess, all their apparel must be changed, and every hair of their body shaven off with a sharp razor, lest they secrete magical charms to prevent their confessing. Witches are most apt to confess on Fridays.

In England, Witchcraft has been chiefly confined to women; the reason assigned is, that the Devil having experienced, in the temptation of Eve, the facility with which that sex are led astray—and also found that, when they once deviate from the paths of virtue, they become more wicked than men—he therefore makes his attacks on them, in preference to the other sex.

Not only women, but even little children, have been convicted of Witchcraft in Sweden, as may be seen in the account printed in Glanvil.

Some hair, the parings of the nails, and urine, of any person bewitched—or, as the term is, labouring under an evil tongue—being put into a stone bottle, with crooked nails, corked close, and tied down with wire, and hung up the chimney, will cause the Witch to suffer the most acute torments imaginable, till the bottle is uncorked, and the mixture dispersed; insomuch that they will even risk a detection, by coming to the house, and attempting to pull down the bottle.

On meeting a supposed Witch, it is adviseable to take the wall of her in a town or street, and the right hand of her in a lane or field; and, whilst passing her, to clench both hands, doubling the thumbs beneath the fingers: this will prevent her having a power to injure the person so doing at that time. It is well to salute a Witch with civil words, on meeting her, before she speaks. But no presents of apples, eggs, or any other thing, should be received from her on any account.

Some persons, born at particular times, and under certain combinations of the planets, have the power of distinguishing Witches at first sight. One of these persons, named Mathew Hopkins, of Manningtree, in Essex, with a John Stern, and a woman in their company, were, in 1644, permitted to go round, from town to town, through most parts of Essex, Suffolk, and Huntingdonshire, with a sort of commission to discover Witches; nay, it is said, were paid twenty shillings for each town they visited. Many persons were pitched upon by them, and through their means convicted. Till at length some gentlemen, out of indignation at Hopkins's barbarity, tied him in the manner he had bound others, that is, thumbs and toes together; in which state, putting him into the water, he swam. This cleared the country of them.

The following statute, enacted the 1st of King James I. will shew that the belief of most of the articles here related was not confined to the populace; nor was it repealed till the 9th year of the reign of King George I.

'Any one that shall use, practise, or exercise any invocation or conjuration of any evil or wicked spirit, or consult, covenant with, entertaine or employ, feede or reward, any evil or wicked spirit, to or for any intent or purpose; or take up any dead man, woman, or child, out of his, her, or their grave, or any other place where the dead body resteth, or the skin, bone, or other part of any dead person, to be employed or used in any manner of witchcraft, sorcery, charme, or enchantment; or shall use, practise, or exercise any witchcraft, enchantment, charme, or sorcery, whereby any person shall be killed, destroyed, wasted, consumed, pined, or lamed, in his or her body, or any part thereof, such offenders, duly and lawfully convicted and attainted, shall suffer death.

'If any person shall take upon him, by witchcraft, enchantment, charme, or sorcery, to tell or declare in what place any treasure of gold or silver should or might be found or had in the earth, or other secret places, or where goods or things lost or stolen should be found or become; or to the intent to provoke any person to unlawful love; or whereby any cattell or goods of any person shall be destroyed, wasted, or impaired; or to destroy or hurt any person in his or her body, though the same be not effected, &c. a yeare's imprisonment and pillory, &c. and the second conviction, death.'

A Sorcerer, or Magician

A Sorcerer, or Magician, differs from a witch in this: A witch derives all her power from a compact with the Devil; a Sorcerer commands him, and the infernal spirits, by his skill in powerful charms and invocations; and also soothes and entices them by fumigations: for the devils are observed to have delicate nostrils, abominating and flying some kinds of stinks; witness the flight of the evil spirit into the remote parts of Egypt, driven by the smell of a fish's liver burned by Tobit. They are also found to be peculiarly fond of certain perfumes; insomuch that Lilly informs us that one Evans, having raised a spirit, at the request of Lord Bothwell and Sir Kenelm Digby, and forgetting a suffumigation, the spirit, vexed at the disappointment, snatched him from out his circle, and carried him from his house, in the Minories, into a field near Battersea Causeway.

King James, in his Daemonologia, says, 'The art of sorcery consists in diverse forms of circles and conjurations rightly joined together, few or more in number, according to the number of persons conjurors (alwaies passing the singular number), according to the qualitie of the circle, and form of the apparition. Two principall things cannot well in that errand be wanted: holy water (whereby the Devill mockes the papists), and some present of a living thing unto him. There are likewise certaine daies and houres that they observe in this purpose. These things being all ready and prepared, circles are made, triangular, quadrangular, round, double, or single, according to the forme of the apparition they crave. But to speake of the diverse formes of the circles, of the innumerable characters and crosses that are within and without, and out-through the same; of the diverse formes of apparitions that the craftie spirit illudes them with, and of all such particulars in that action, I remit it to over many that have busied their heads in describing of the same, as being but curious, and altogether unprofitable. And this farre only I touch, that, when the conjured spirit appears, which will not be while after many circumstances, long prayers, and much muttering and murmurings of the conjurors, like a papist priest dispatching a hunting masse—how soone, I say, he appeares, if they have missed one jote of all their rites; or if any of their feete once slyd over the circle, through terror of his fearfull apparition, he paies himself at that time, in his owne hand, of that due debt which they ought him, and otherwise would have delaicd longer to have paied him: I mean, he carries them with him, body and soule. If this be not now a just cause to make them weary of these formes of conjuration, I leave it to you to judge upon; considering the longsomeness of the labour, the precise keeping of daies and houres (as I have said), the terribleness of the apparition, and the present peril that they stand in, in missing the least circumstance or freite that they ought to observe: and, on the other part, the Devill is glad to moove them to a plaine and square dealing with him, as I said before.'

This is a pretty accurate description of this mode of conjuration, styled the Circular Method; but, with all due respect to his Majesty's learning, square and triangular circles are figures not to be found in Euclid, or any of the common writers on geometry. But, perhaps. King James learned his mathematics from the same system as Doctor Sacheverell, who, in one of his speeches or sermons, made use of the following simile: 'They concur like parallel lines meeting in one common center.'

Another mode of consulting spirits was by the berryl, by means of a speculator or seer; who, to have a complete sight, ought to be a pure virgin, a youth who had not known woman, or at least a person of irreproachable life and purity of manners. The method of such consultation is this: The conjuror having repeated the necessary charms and adjurations, with the Litany, or invocation peculiar to the spirits or angels he wishes to call (for every one has his particular form), the seer looks into a chrystal or berryl, wherein he will see the answer, represented either by types or figures; and sometimes, though very rarely, will hear the angels or spirits speak articulately. Their pronunciation is, as Lilly says, like the Irish, much in the throat.

Lilly describes one of these berryls or chrystals. It was, he says, as large as an orange, set in silver, with a cross at the top, and round about engraved the names of the angels Raphael, Gabriel, and Uriel. A delineation of another is engraved in the frontispiece to Aubery's Miscellanies.

This mode of enquiry was practised by Doctor Dee, the celebrated mathematician: his speculator was named Kelly. From him, and others practising this art, we have a long muster-roll of the infernal host, their different natures, tempers, and appearances. Doctor Reginald Scot has given a list of some of the chiefs of these devils or spirits, of which I shall here set down two or three, which, I dare say, the Reader will think fully sufficient.

'Their first and principal king (which is the Power of the East), is called *Baell*, who, when he is conjured up, appeareth with three heads; the first like a toad, the second like a man, the third like a cat. He speaketh with a hoarse voice; he maketh a man to go invisible. He hath under his obedience and rule sixty-and-six legions of devils.

'The first duke under the Power of the East, is named *Agares*. He cometh up mildly, in the likeness of a fair old man, riding upon a crocodile, and carrying a hawk on his fist. He teacheth presently all manner of tongues; he fetcheth back all such as run away, and maketh them run that stand still; he overthroweth all dignities supernatural and temporal; he maketh earthquakes: and is of the order of virtues, having under his regiment thirty-one legions.

'*Marbas*, alias *Barbas*, is a great president, and appeareth in the form of a mighty lion; but, at the commandment of a conjurer, cometh up in the likeness of a man, and answereth fully as touching any thing that is hidden or secret. He bringeth diseases, and cureth them; he promoteth wisdom, and the knowledge of mechanical arts, or handicrafts; he changeth men into other shapes; and under his presidency or government are thirty-six legions of devils contained.'

These Sorcerers or Magicians do not always employ their art to do mischief; but, on the contrary, frequently exert it to cure diseases inflicted by witches; to discover thieves; recover stolen goods; to foretel future events, and the state of absent friends. On this account, they are frequently called White Witches.

Fairies

THIS PIECE OF Superstition seems to come from the East, and was probably imported into Europe by some of the Crusaders; as this kind of spirits, in many instances, resembles the genii, of whom so many wonderful stories are told by the Arabians; though some derive them from the lares and larvae of the Romans.

Fairies, according to the popular accounts of them, are a sort of intermediate beings between men and spirits; having bodies, with the power of rendering them invisible, and of passing them through all sorts of inclosures. They are remarkably small of stature, with fair complexions, whence they obtained the name of Fairies. Both male and female are generally clothed in green; and frequent groves, mountains, the southern sides of hills, and green meadows, where they amuse themselves with dancing, hand in hand, in a circle, by moonlight. The traces of their feet are visible next morning on the grass, and are commonly called Fairy Rings, or Circles.

Fairies appear to have all the passions and wants of men; but are great lovers of cleanliness and propriety, for the observance of which they frequently reward servants, by dropping money in their shoes: they likewise severely punish sluts and slovens, by pinching them black and blue. Lilly says they are likewise friends to persons of strict diet, of an upright life, and using fervent prayers to God. Fairies are particularly fond of making cakes; in the doing of which they are said to be very noisy. In Ireland, they frequently lay bannocks, a kind of oaten cakes, in the way of travellers over the mountains; and if they do not accept of the intended favour, and eat the bannock, or at least take it up, they seldom escape a hearty beating, or something worse.

Fairies oft change their weakly and starveling elves, or children, for the more robust offspring of men. But this can only be done before baptism; for which reason it is still the custom, in the Highlands, to watch by the cradles of infants most assiduously till they are christened. Children so changed have been kept for seven years. There are divers methods of discovering whether a child belongs to the Fairies or not. One is given in the following story, printed in a book intitled, A pleasant Treatise on Witchcraft.

'A certain woman having put out her child to nurse in the country, found, when she came to take it home, that its form was so much altered that she scarce knew it: nevertheless, not knowing what time might do, took it home for her own. But when, after some years, it could neither speak nor go, the poor woman was fain to carry it, with much trouble, in her arms: and one day, a poor man coming to the door, "God bless you, Mistress," said he, "and your poor child; be pleased to bestow something on a poor man." "Ah! this child," replied she, "is the cause of all my sorrow:" and related what had happened; adding, moreover, that she thought it changed, and none of her child. The old man, whom years had rendered more prudent in such matters, told her, that, to find out the truth she should make a clear fire, sweep the hearth very clean, and place the child fast in his chair, that he might not fall, before it; then break a dozen eggs, and place the four-and-twenty half shells before it; then go out, and listen at the door: for, if the child spoke, it was certainly a changeling: and then she should carry it out, and leave it on the dunghill to cry, and not to pity it, till she heard its voice no more. The woman, having done all things according to these words, heard the child say, "Seven years old was I before I came to the nurse, and four years have I lived since, and never saw so many milk-pans before." So the woman took it up, and left it upon the dunghill to cry, and not to be pitied; till at last she thought the voice went up into the air: and coming, found there her own natural and well-favoured child.'—The very term Changeling, now used to signify one almost an idiot, bears testimony to the current belief of these changes. As all the Fairy children were little, backward of their tongue, and seemingly idiots; therefore stunted and idiotical children were supposed changelings.

Some Fairies dwell in the mines, and seem to imitate the actions of the workmen; but never, unless insulted, do them harm, but rather are of service to them. In certain silver and lead mines, in Wales, nothing is more common than these subterraneous spirits, called Knockers, who good-naturedly point out where there is a rich vein. These Knockers are sometimes visible. Mr. John Lewis, in his correspondence with Mr. Baxter, describes them as little-statured, and about half a yard long; and adds, that at this very instant there are miners on a discovery of a vein of metal on his own lands, and that two of them are ready to make oath they heard these Knockers in the day-time.

In Scotland there were a sort of domestic Fairies, from their sun-burnt complexions called Brownies: these were extremely useful performing all sorts of domestic drudgery.

Fairies sometimes shoot at cattle, with arrows headed with flint-stones; these are often found, and are called elf-shots. In order to effect the cure of an animal so injured, it is to be touched with one of these elf-shots, or to be made drink the water in which one has been dipped.

The Second-Sight

THE SECOND-SIGHT IS so called from its being a supplemental faculty of sight, added to that of common vision; whereby certain appearances, predictive of future events, present themselves suddenly and spontaneously before persons so gifted, without any endeavour or desire on their part to see them.

Accounts differ much respecting this faculty; some make it hereditary, which is denied by others. The same difference arises respecting the power of communicating it. But, according to an account from a gentleman at Strathspay to Mr. Aubrey, some of the Seers acknowledged the possibility of teaching it. This gift, or faculty, is in general rather troublesome than agreeable to the possessors of it, who are chiefly found among the inhabitants of the Highlands of Scotland, those of the Western Isles, of the Isle of Man, and of Ireland. The account sent to Mr. Aubrey says, 'In the Isle of Sky, especially before the Gospel came thither, several families had it by succession, descending from parents to children; and as yet there are many that have it that way: and the only way to be freed from it is, when a woman hath it herself, and is married to a man that hath it also, if, in the very act of delivery, upon the first sight of the child's head, it be baptized, the same is free from it; if not, he hath it all his life.'

These visions are not confined to solemn or important events. The future visit of a mountebank, or piper; a plentiful draught of fish; the arrival of common travellers; or, if possible, still more trifling matters than these, are foreseen by the Seers.

Not only aged men and women have the Second-Sight, but also children, horses, and cows. Children, endowed with that faculty, manifest it by crying aloud, at the very time that a corpse appears to a Seer: of this many instances could be given. That horses possess, it, is likewise plain, from their violent and sudden starting when their rider, or a Seer in company with him, sees a vision of any kind, by night or by day. It is observable of a horse, that he will not go forwards towards the apparition, but must be led round, at some distance from the common road; his terror is evident from his becoming all over in a profuse sweat, although quite cool a moment before. Balaam's ass seems to have possessed this power, or faculty; and, perhaps, what we improperly style a startlish horse, may be one who has the gift of the Second-Sight. That cows have the Second-Sight, is proved by the following circumstance: If a woman, whilst milking a cow, happen to have a vision of that kind, the cow runs away in a great fright at the same instant, and cannot, for some time, be brought to stand quietly.

To judge of the meaning of many visions, or the time in which they will be accomplished, requires observation and experience. In general, the time of accomplishment bears some relation to the time of the day in which they are seen. Thus, visions seen early in the morning (which seldom happens), will be much sooner accomplished than those appearing at noon; and those seen at noon, will take place in a much shorter time than those happening at night: sometimes the accomplishment of the last does not fall out within a year or more.

The appearance of a person wrapt in a shroud, is, in general, a prognostic of the death of the party. The time when it will happen, may be judged from the height it reaches; for if it be not seen above the middle, death is not to be expected for a year or more: but when the shroud appears closed about the head, the accomplishment is not many hours distant.

If, in a vision, a woman is seen standing near a man's left hand, she will become his wife; if there are two or three about him, he will marry them all in succession, according to their proximity. A spark of fire, falling on the belly of a married woman, predicts her delivery of a dead child; the like spark, falling on her arm, betokens she shall shortly carry a dead child.

If a seat, in which a person is sitting, suddenly appears empty, although he hath not moved, this is a certain presage that such person will very shortly die.

Persons who have not long been gifted with Second-Sight, after seeing a vision without doors, on coming into a house, and approaching the fire, will immediately fall into a swoon. All those that have the Second-Sight, do not see these appearances at the same time; but if one having this faculty designedly touches his fellow Seer, at the instant that a vision appears to him, in that case it will be seen by both.

During the appearance of a vision, the eyelids of some of the Seers are so erected and distended, that they cannot close them otherwise than by drawing them down with their fingers, or by employing others to do it for them.

Omens Portending Death

The howling of a dog is a certain sign that some one of the family will very shortly die.

A screech owl slapping its wings against the windows of a sick person's chamber, or screeching at them, portends the same.

Three loud and distinct knocks at the bed's head of a sick person, or at the bed's head or door of any of his relations, is an Omen of his death.

A drop of blood from the nose, commonly foretels death, or a very severe fit of sickness: three drops are still more ominous.

Rats gnawing the hangings of a room, is reckoned the forerunner of a death in the family.

Breaking a looking-glass betokens a mortality in the family, commonly the master.

Is the neck of a dead child remains flexible for several hours after its decease, it portends that some person in that house will die in a short time.

A coal in the shape of a coffin, flying out of the fire to any particular person, betokens their death not far off.

A collection of tallow rising up against the wick of a candle, is styled a Winding Sheet, and deemed an omen of death in the family.

Besides these general notices, many families have particular warnings or notices; some by the appearance of a bird, and others by the figure of a tall woman, dressed all in white, that goes shrieking about the house. This apparition is common in Ireland, where it is called Ben-Shea, and the Shrieking Woman.

Mr. Pennant says, that many of the great families in Scotland had their daemon, or genius, who gave them monitions of future events. Thus the family of Rothmurchas had the Bodach an dun, or the Ghost of the Hill; Kinchardines, the Spectre of the Bloody Hand. Gartinbeg house was haunted by Bodach Gartin; and Tullock Gorms by Maug Monlach, or the Girl with the Hairy Left Hand. The synod gave frequent orders that enquiry should be made into the truth of this apparition; and one or two declared that they had seen one that answered the description.

Corpse Candles are very common appearances in the counties of Cardigan, Carmarthen, and Pembroke, and also in some other parts of

Wales. They are called Candles, from their resemblance, not of the body of the candle, but the fire; because that fire, says the honest Welshman, Mr. Davis, in a letter to Mr. Baxter, doth as much resemble material candle-lights, as eggs do eggs; saving that, in their journey, these candles are sometimes visible, and sometimes disappear; especially if any one comes near to them, or in the way to meet them. On these occasions they vanish, but presently appear again behind the observer, and hold on their course. If a little candle is seen, of a pale or bluish colour, then follows the corpse, either of an abortive, or some infant; if a large one, then the corpse of some one come to age. If there be seen two, three, or more, of different sizes—some big, some small—then shall so many corpses pass together, and of such ages, or degrees. If two candles come from different places, and be seen to meet, the corpses will do the same; and if any of these candles be seen to turn aside, through some bye path leading to the church, the following corpse will be found to take exactly the same way.

Sometimes these Candles point out the places where persons shall sicken and die. They have also appeared on the bellies of pregnant women, previous to their delivery; and predicted the drowning of persons passing a ford. All these appearances have been seen by a number of persons ready to give their testimony of the truth thereof, some within three weeks of Mr. Davis's writing the letter here quoted.

Another kind of fiery apparition peculiar to Wales, is what is called the *Tan-we*, or *Tan-wed*. This appeareth, says Mr. Davis, to our seeming, in the lower region of the air, straight and long, not much unlike a glaive; mours or shoots directly and level (as who should say, I'll hit), but far more slowly than falling stars. It lighteneth all the air and ground where it passeth, lasteth three or four miles, or more, for aught is known, because no man seeth the rising or beginning of it; and, when it falls to the ground, it sparkleth, and lighteth all about. These commonly announce the decease of freeholders, by falling on their lands: and you shall scarce bury any such with us, says Mr. Davis, be he but a lord of a house and garden, but you shall find some one at his burial, that hath seen this fire fall on some part of his lands. Sometimes those appearances have been seen by the persons whose death they foretold; two instances of which Mr. Davis records, as having happened in his own family.

The clicking of a death-watch is an omen of the death of some one in the house wherein it is heard.

A Child, who does not cry when sprinkled in baptism, will not live.

Children prematurely wise are not long-lived, that is, rarely reach maturity. This notion is quoted by Shakespeare, and put into the mouth of Richard III. Fond parents are, however, apt to terrify themselves, on this occasion, without any great cause: witness the mother, who gave as an instance of the uncommon sense of her boy, of only six years of age. That he having laid his dear little hand on a red-hot poker, took it away, without any one soul alive bidding him.

Charms and Ceremonies for Knowing Future Events

ANY PERSON FASTING on Midsummer eve, and sitting in the church porch, will at midnight see the spirits of the persons of that parish, who will die that year, come and knock at the church door, in the order and succession in which they will die. One of these watchers, there being several in company, fell into a sound sleep, so that he could not be waked: whilst in this state, his ghost or spirit was seen by the rest of his companions, knocking at the church door. See *Pandemonium,* by R. B.

Any unmarried woman fasting on Midsummer eve, and at midnight laying a clean cloth, with bread, cheese, and ale, and sitting down, as if going to eat, the street door being left open—the person whom she is afterwards to marry will come into the room, and drink to her by bowing; and afterwards filling the glass, will leave it on the table, and, making another bow, retire. See *Pandemonium*.

On St. Agnes night, 21st of January, take a row of pins, and pull out every one, one after another, saying a Pater-noster on sticking a pin in your sleeve, and you will dream of him or her you shall marry.

Another method to see a future spouse in a dream:—The party enquiring must lie in a different county from that in which he commonly resides; and, on going to bed, must knit the left garter about the right-legged stocking, letting the other garter and stocking alone; and, as you rehearse the following verses, at every comma knit a knot:

> This knot I knit,
> To know the thing I know not yet;
> That I may see
> The man (woman) that shall my husband (wife) be;
> How he goes, and what he wears,
> And what he does all days and years.

Accordingly, in a dream, he will appear, with the insignia of his trade or profession.

Another, performed by charming the Moon, thus:—At the first appearance of the New Moon, immediately after the new year's day (though some say any other New Moon is as good), go out in the evening, and stand over the spars of a gate or stile, and, looking on the Moon, repeat the following lines:

All hail to the Moon ! all hail to thee!
I prithee, good Moon, reveal to me,
This night, who my husband (wife) must be.

The person must presently after go to bed, when they will dream of the person destined for their future husband or wife.

A slice of the bride-cake, thrice drawn through the wedding ring, and laid under the head of an unmarried man or woman, will make them dream of their future wife or husband. The same is practised in the North with a piece of the groaning cheese.

To discover a thief by the sieve and sheers: Stick the points of the sheers in the wood of the sieve, and let two persons support it, balanced upright, with their two fingers: then read a certain chapter in the Bible, and afterwards ask St. Peter and St. Paul, if A. or B. is the thief, naming all the persons you suspect. On naming the real thief, the sieve will turn suddenly round about.

Superstitious Cures and Preventatives

A SLUNK OR ABORTIVE calf, buried in the highway over which cattle frequently pass, will greatly prevent that misfortune happening to cows. This is commonly practised in Suffolk.

A ring made of the hinge of a coffin is supposed to have the virtue of preventing the cramp.

Certain herbs, stones, and other substances, as also particular words written on parchment, as a charm, have the property of preserving men from wounds in the midst of a battle or engagement. This was so universally credited, that an oath was administered to persons going to fight a legal duel, 'That they had ne charm, ne herb of virtue.' The power of rendering themselves invulnerable, is still believed by the Germans; it is performed by divers charms and ceremonies; and so firm is their belief of its efficacy, that they will rather attribute any hurt they may receive, after its performance, to some omission in the performance, than defect in its virtue.

A halter wherewith any one has been hanged, if tied about the head, will cure the head-ach.

Moss growing on a human skull, if dried, powdered, and taken as snuff, will cure the head-ach.

A dead man's hand is supposed to have the quality of dispelling tumours, such as wens, or swelled glands, by stroking with it, nine times, the place affected. It seems as if the hand of a person dying a violent death was deemed particularly efficacious; as it very frequently happens, that nurses bring children to be stroked with the hands of executed criminals, even whilst they are hanging on the gallows.

Touching a dead body, prevents dreaming of it.

The word ABACADABARA, written asunder, and worn about the neck, will cure an ague:

> A B A C A D A B A R A
> B A C A D A B A R
> A C A D A B A
> C A D A B
> A D A
> D

To cure warts:—Steal a piece of beef from a butcher's shop, and rub your warts with it; then throw it down the necessary house, or bury it; and, as the beef rots, your warts will decay.

The chips or cuttings of a gibbet or gallows, on which one or more persons have been executed or exposed, if worn next the skin, or round the neck, in a bag, will cure the ague, or prevent it.

A stone with a hole in it, hung at the bed's head, will prevent the night-mare: it is therefore called a hag-stone, from that disorder, which is occasioned by a hag, or witch, sitting on the stomach of the party afflicted. It also prevents witches riding horses; for which purpose it is often tied to a stable key.

If a tree, of any kind, is split—and weak, ricketty, or ruptured children drawn through it, and afterwards the tree is bound together, so as to make it unite—as the tree heals, and grows together, so will the child acquire strength. Sir John Cullum, who saw this operation twice performed, thus describes it: 'For this purpose a young ash was each time selected, and split longitudinally about five feet: the fissure was kept wide open by my gardener; whilst the friend of the child, having first stripped him naked, passed him thrice through it, always head foremost. As soon as the operation was performed, the wounded tree was bound up with a packthread; and, as the bark healed, the child was to recover. The first of the young patients was to be cured of the rickets, the second of a rupture.' This is a very ancient and extensive piece of superstition.—Creeping through tolmen, or perforated stones, was a Druidical ceremony, and is practised in the East Indies. Mr. Borlace mentions a stone, in the parish of Marden, having a hole in it, fourteen inches diameter; through which many persons have crept, for pains in their backs and limbs; and many children have been drawn, for the rickets. In the North, children are drawn through a hole cut in the groaning cheese, on the day they are christened.

Sympathy

THE WOUNDS OF a murdered person will bleed afresh, on the body being touched, ever so lightly, in any part, by the murderer.

A person being suddenly taken with a shivering, is a sign that some one has just then walked over the spot of their future grave. Probably all persons are not subject to this sensation; otherwise the inhabitants of those parishes, whose burial grounds lie in the common foot-path, would live in one continual fit of shaking.

When a person's cheek, or ear, burns, it is a sign that some one is then talking of him or her. If it is the right cheek, or ear, the discourse is to their advantage; if the left, to their disadvantage.

When the right eye itches, the party affected will shortly cry; if the left, they will laugh.

Things Lucky and Unlucky

IT IS CUSTOMARY for women to offer to sit cross-legged, to procure luck at cards for their friends. Sitting cross-legged, with the fingers interlaced, was anciently esteemed a magical posture.

It is deemed lucky to be born with a caul, or membrane, over the face. This is an ancient and general Superstition. In France, it is proverbial: *etre né coiffée*, is an expression signifying that a person is extremely fortunate. This caul is esteemed an infallible preservative against drowning; and, under that idea, is frequently advertised for sale in our public papers, and purchased by seamen. It is related that midwives used to sell this membrane to advocates, as an especial means of making them eloquent: and one Protus was accused by the clergy of Constantinople with having offended in this article. According to Chrysostom, the midwives frequently sold it for magical uses.

A person possessed of a caul may know the state of health of the party who was born with it: if alive and well, it is firm and crisp; if dead or sick, relaxed and flaccid.

It is reckoned a good omen, or a sign of future happiness, if the sun shines on a couple coming out of the church after having been married. It is also esteemed a good sign is it rains whilst a corpse is burying:

> Happy is the bride that the sun shines on;
> Happy is the corpse that the rain rains on.

To break a looking-glass is extremely unlucky; the party to whom it belongs will lose his best friend.

If, going a journey on business, a sow cross the road, you will probably meet with a disappointment, if not a bodily accident, before you return home. To avert this, you must endeavour to prevent her crossing you; and if that cannot be done, you must ride round on fresh ground. Is the sow is attended with her litter of pigs, it is lucky, and denotes a successful journey.

It is unlucky to see, first one magpye, and then more; but to see two, denotes marriage or merriment; three, a successful journey; four, an unexpected piece of good news; five, you will shortly be in a great company. To kill a magpye, will certainly be punished with some terrible misfortune.

If, in a family, the youngest daughter should be married before her elder sisters, they must all dance at her wedding without shoes: this will counteract their ill luck, and procure them husbands.

If you meet a funeral procession, or one passes by you, always take off your hat: this keeps all evil spirits attending the body in good humour.

If, in eating, you miss your mouth, and the victuals fall, it is very unlucky, and denotes approaching sickness.

It is supposed extremely unlucky to have a dead body on board of a ship at sea.

Children are deemed lucky to a ship; their innocence being, by the sailors, supposed a protection.

It is lucky to put on a stocking the wrong side outwards: changing it, alters the luck.

When a person goes out to transact any important business, it is lucky to throw an old shoe after him.

It is lucky to tumble up stairs: probably this is a jocular observation, meaning, it was lucky the party did not tumble down stairs.

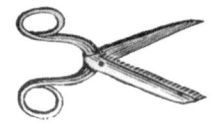

It is unlucky to present a knife, scissors, razor, or any sharp or cutting instrument, to one's mistress or friend, as they are apt to cut love and friendship. To avoid the ill effects of this, a pin, a farthing, or some trifling recompence, must be taken. To find a knife or razor, denotes ill luck and disappointment to the party.

It is unlucky to walk under a ladder; it may prevent your being married that year.

It is a common practice among the lower class of hucksters, pedlars, or dealers in fruit or fish, on receiving the price of the first goods sold that day, which they call hansel, to spit on the money, as they term it, for good luck: and boxers, before they set to, commonly spit in their hands, which was originally done for luck's sake.

The first time a nurse brings a child to visit its parents or relations, it is unlucky to send it back without some gift, as eggs, salt, or bread.

It is held extremely unlucky to kill a cricket, a lady-bug, a swallow, martin, robin-red-breast, or wren; perhaps from the idea of its being a breach of hospitality; all those birds and insects taking refuge in houses.

There is a particular distich in favour of the robin and wren:

A robin and a wren
Are God Almighty's cock and hen.

Persons killing any of the above-mentioned birds or insects, or destroying their nests, will infallibly, within the course of the year, break a bone, or meet with some other dreadful misfortune. On the contrary, it is deemed lucky to have martins or swallows build their nests in the eaves of a house, or on the chimneys.

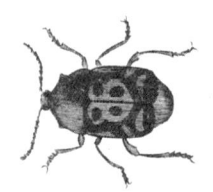

It is unlucky to lay one's knife and fork crosswise: crosses and misfortunes are likely to follow.

Many persons have certain days of the week and month on which they are particularly fortunate, and others in which they are as generally unlucky: these days are different to different persons. Mr. Aubrey has given several instances of both in divers persons. Some days, however, are commonly deemed unlucky: among others, Friday labours under that opprobrium; and it is pretty generally held, that no new work or enterprize should be commenced on that day. Likewise respecting the weather, there is this proverb:

> Friday's moon,
> Come when it will, it comes too soon.

Washing hands in the same bason, or with the same water, as another person has washed in, is extremely unlucky, as the parties will infallibly quarrel.

To scatter salt, by overturning the vessel in which it is contained, is very unlucky, and portends quarrelling with a friend, or fracture of a bone, sprain, or other bodily misfortune. Indeed this may in some measure be averted, by throwing a small quantity of it over one's head. It is also unlucky to help another person to salt; to whom the ill luck is to happen, does not seem to be settled.

Whistling at sea is supposed to cause an increase of wind, if not a storm, and therefore much disliked by seamen; though, sometimes, they themselves practise it when there is a dead calm.

Drowning a cat at sea, is extremely unlucky.

Miscellaneous Superstitions

THE PASSING-BELL WAS anciently rung for two purposes: one, to bespeak the prayers of all good Christians for a soul just departing; the other, to drive away the evil spirits who stood at the bed's-foot, and about the house, ready to seize their prey, or at least to molest and terrify the soul in its passage: but by the ringing of that bell (for Durandus informs us, evil spirits are much afraid of bells), they were kept aloof; and the soul, like a hunted hare, gained the start, or had what is by sportsmen called Law. Hence, perhaps, exclusive of the additional labour, was occasioned the high price demanded for tolling the greatest bell of the church; for, that being louder, the evil spirits must go farther off to be clear of its sound, by which the poor soul got so much more the start of them: besides, being heard farther off, it would likewise procure the dying man a greater number of prayers. This dislike of spirits to bells, is mentioned in the

Golden Legend, by W. de Worde. 'It is said, the evill spirytes that ben in the regyon of thayre, doubte moche when they here the belles rongen: and this is the cause why the belles ben rongen whan it thondreth, and whan grete tempeste and outrages of wether happen, to the ende that the feindes and wycked spirytes shold be abashed and flee, and cease of the movynge of tempeste.'

The toad has a stone in its head, very efficacious in the cure of divers diseases; but it must be taken out of the animal whilst alive.

The ass has a cross on its back, ever since Christ rode on one of these animals.

The haddock has the mark of St. Peter's thumb, ever since St. Peter took the tribute penny out of the mouth of a fish of that species.

Most persons break the shells of eggs, after they have eaten the meat. This was originally done to prevent their being used as boats by witches.

A coal hopping out of the fire, in the shape of a purse, predicts a sudden acquisition of riches to the person near whom it falls.

A flake of soot hanging at the bars of the grate, denotes the visit of a stranger from that part of the country nearest the object: a kind of fungus in the candle predicts the same.

A spark in the candle denotes that the party opposite to it will shortly receive a letter.

In setting a hen, the good women hold it an indispensable rule to put an odd number of eggs.

All sorts of remedies are directed to be taken three, seven, or nine times. Salutes with cannon consist of an odd number; a royal salute is thrice seven, or twenty-one guns. This predilection for odd numbers is very ancient, and is mentioned by Virgil in the eighth Eclogue, where many spells and charms, still practised, are recorded; but, not-withstanding these opinions in savour of odd numbers, the number thirteen is considered as extremely ominous; it being held that, when thirteen persons meet in a room, one of them will die within the year.

It is impossible for a person to die whilst resting on a pillow stuffed with the feathers of a dove; but they will struggle with death in most exquisite torture. The pillows of dying persons are therefore frequently taken away, when they appear in great agonies, lest they may have pigeons feathers in them.

Fern seed is looked on as having great magical powers, and must be gathered on midsummer eve. A person who went to gather it, reported that the spirits whisked by his ears, and sometimes struck his hat, and other parts of his body; and at length, when he thought he had got a good quantity of it, and secured it in papers and a box, when he came home, he found both empty. See *Pandemonium*.

Any one wounded by a small fish, called a Sting Ray, which often happens in catching sand-eels, will feel the pain of the wound very severely till the next tide.

The Reverend Mr. Shaw, in the History of the Province of Moray, in Scotland, says, 'When a corpse is lifted, the bed of straw, on which the deceased lay, is carried out, and burnt, in a place where no beast can come near it: and they pretend to find next morning, in the ashes, the print of the foot of the person in the family who shall first die.'

Although the devil can partly transform himself into a variety of shapes, he cannot change his cloven foot, which will always mark him under every appearance.

A manuscript in the Cotton Library, marked Julius, F. 6, has the following superstitions, practised in the lordship of Gasborough, in Cleveland, Yorkshire:

Any one whistling, after it is dark, or daylight is closed, must go thrice about the house, by way of penance. How this whistling becomes criminal, is not said.

When any one dieth, certain women sing a song to the dead body, reciting the journey that the party deceased must go.

They esteem it necessary to give, once in their lives, a pair of new shoes to a poor person; believing that, after their decease, they shall be obliged to pass bare-foot over a great space of ground, or heath, overgrown with thorns and furzes; unless, by such gift, they have redeemed this obligation: in which case, when they come to the edge of this heath, an old man will meet them, with the self-same pair of shoes they have given; by the help of which they will pass over unhurt: that is, provided the shoes have no holes in them; a circumstance the fabricator of the tale forgot to stipulate.

When a maid takes the pot off the fire, she sets it down in great haste, and with her hands stops the pot-hooks from vibrating; believing that our lady greeteth (that is, weepeth) all the time the pot-hooks are in motion.

Between the towns of Aten and Newton, near the foot of Rosberrye Toppinge, there is a well dedicated to St. Oswald. The neighbours have an opinion, that a shirt, or shift, taken off a sick person, and thrown into that well, will shew whether the person will recover, or die: for if it floated, it denoted the recovery of the party; if it sunk, there remained no hope of their life: and, to reward the Saint for his intelligence, they tear off a rag of the shirt, and leave it hanging on the briars thereabouts; 'where,' says the writer, 'I have seen such numbers, as might have made a fayre rheme in a paper myll.' These wells, called Rag-wells, were formerly not uncommon. Something like them is mentioned by Mr. Hanway, in his Travels in Persia, vol. i. p. 177; where he says, 'After ten days journey, we arrived at a desolate carravansera, where we found nothing but water. I observed a tree with a number of rags tied to the branches: these were so many charms, which passengers coming from Ghilan, a province remarkable for agues, had left there, in a fond expectation of leaving this disease also on the same spot.' The Reverend Mr. Brand, in his ingenious Annotations on Bourne's Popular Antiquities, mentions a well of this kind at Benton, in the neighbourhood of Newcastle.

Mr. Pennant tells us of two in Scotland: these were visited for many distempers, where the offerings were small pieces of money, and bits of rags.

The fishermen every year change their companions, for luck's sake. On St. Peter's day they new paint their boats, and give a treat to their friends and neighbours; at which they sprinkle their boats with ale, observing certain ceremonies.

The seventh son of a seventh son is born a physician; having an intuitive knowledge of the art of curing all disorders, and sometimes the faculty of performing wonderful cures by touching only.

To conclude this article, and my book, I shall transcribe a foreign piece of Superstition, firmly believed in many parts of France, Germany, and Spain. The account of it, and the mode of preparation, appears to have been given by a judge; in the latter, there is a striking resemblance to the charm in Macbeth.

Of the Hand of Glory, which is made use of by housebreakers, to enter into houses at night, without fear of opposition.

I ACKNOWLEDGE THAT I never tried the secret of the Hand of Glory, but I have thrice assisted at the definitive judgment of certain criminals, who, under the torture, confessed having used it. Being asked what it was, how they procured it, and what were its uses and properties?—they answered, first, that the use of the Hand of Glory was to stupify those to whom it was presented, and to render them motionless, insomuch that they could not stir, any more than if they were dead; secondly, that it was the hand of a hanged man; and thirdly, that it must be prepared in the manner following:

Take the hand, left or right, of a person hanged, and exposed on the highway; wrap it up in a piece of a shroud, or winding sheet, in which let it be well squeezed, to get out any small quantity of blood that may have remained in it; then put it into an earthen vessel, with zimat, saltpetre, salt, and long pepper, the whole well powdered; leave it fifteen days in that vessel; afterwards take it out, and expose it to the noontide sun in the dog days, till it is thoroughly dry; and if the sun is not sufficient, put it into an oven heated with fern and vervain: then compose a kind of candle with the fat of a hanged man, virgin wax, and sisame of Lapland. The Hand of Glory is used as a candlestick to hold this candle, when lighted. Its properties are, that wheresoever any one goes with this dreadful instrument, the persons to whom it is presented will be deprived of all power of motion. On being asked if there was no remedy, or antidote, to counteract this charm, they said the Hand of Glory would cease to take effect, and thieves could not make use of it, if the threshold of the door of the house, and other places by which they might enter, were anointed with an unguent composed of the gall of a black cat, the fat of a white hen, and the blood of a screech owl; which mixture must necessarily be prepared during the dog days.

FINIS.